Foods from India

Garrett Byrne

PRINCE ALBERT PUBLIC LIBRARY

Series Editor **Anne Taylor**

Level 1 - ❶

Foods from India
Garrett Byrne

© 2022 Seed Learning, Inc.

All rights reserved. No part of this book may be reproduced, stored in a retrieval system, or transmitted in any form by any means, electronic, mechanical, photocopying, recording, or otherwise, without prior permission in writing from the publisher.

Series Editor: Anne Taylor
Acquisitions Editor: Casey Malarcher
Copy Editor: Liana Robinson
Cover/Interior Design: Highline Studio

Library of Congress Control Number: 2021916172

ISBN: 978-1-953705-47-1

10 9 8 7 6 5 4 3 2 1
25 24 23 22

Photo Credits
All photos are © Shutterstock, Inc.

Contents

Delicious Indian Foods 4

Naan 9

Chutney 15

Chai 20

Reading Quiz 27

New Words 28

Menu 30

Notes 32

Delicious Indian Foods

India is in the south of Asia.
It is a very large country!
It has over 1.4 billion people.

INDIA

India is 3,214 km from north to south!

People in India can buy many spices.

Lots of Indian foods

India's foods have many colors!

They also have many spices.

Mint chutney

People in India like chutney.
It is a type of dip.
There are many types of chutney!

Spicy red chutney

Chai made with different spices

A man making chai on the street

Chai is the Indian word for "tea."

You don't need to ask for chai tea.

That is "tea tea!"

Just say, "I'd like some chai!"

Indians love to cook for their families.

They often eat together.

Here are some Indian foods!

Chai, chutney, and naan

A family cooking together

Naan

Naan is a type of flat bread.
It is often cooked in a clay oven.
Naan can be different shapes.

Naan cooked in a clay oven

Naan can be a triangle or a circle.

Eating naan with hands

Use naan like a spoon!

In India, people eat naan with the right hand!
Break the bread with your fingers and thumb.
You can use it instead of a spoon.

Naan and some chutneys

Peshwari naan with nuts and raisins

Naan can come with different ingredients.
Peshwari naan has nuts on top.
You can eat it with some chutney.

Paneer naan is another naan.
Paneer is a type of Indian cheese.
Naan and paneer are great together!

Paneer naan

Paneer

Indian kings and queens ate naan for breakfast.

Long ago, people ate naan for breakfast.
Kings and queens started this.
Soon, others ate it for breakfast, too!
Would you eat naan for breakfast?

Naan for breakfast

Many Indian restaurants are buffet-style.

Now, you can eat naan in most countries. There are Indian restaurants all over the world!

A nice Indian restaurant

Chutney

Chutney is a kind of dip. It can have different ingredients. Chutney can be spicy or not spicy. People eat many foods with chutney.

Some chutney can be hot and spicy!

Samosas and chutneys

15

Red onion chutney

Apple chutney

Spicy tomato chutney

You can make it with fruits or vegetables.

Apple chutney is delicious.

Tomato chutney can be spicy.

← Cilantro chutney is popular in the north.

Coconut chutney → is from the south.

In north India, people like cilantro chutney. In the south, many enjoy coconut chutney.

Three different chutneys

People eat many chutneys together.
This way, they have many dips.
It's fun to have different chutneys together!

A colorful meal with chutneys

Some mango chutney

What chutney would you like?

What would you eat with it?

Chai

Chai is tea made with spices. It also has milk and sugar.

Some white and brown sugar and some milk

Two glasses of chai with spices

Chai is cooked for a long time.
This makes it nice and spicy!

Waiting for tea!

Friends drinking chai together

Chai is part of Indian life. Many Indians drink more than one cup each day. It does not cost much.

A woman drinking chai

Indian money

Chai is good for you!

Chai is very old.

It was made thousands of years ago.

Indians say it's good for you.

A cup of chai

A chai-wallah pouring chai

A glass of chai

People often buy chai on the street.
You can buy some from a *chai-wallah*.
That is what Indians call someone who sells tea.
There are many chai-wallahs around India.

Lots of tea cups

Making chai on the street

Now, many Indians drink two cups a day.
India has over 1.4 billion people.
So, they need many chai-wallahs!

Chai with different spices

Friends drinking chai in the US

Now, people everywhere drink chai.

They like spicy tea.

It's not just for Indians!

Reading Quiz

Choose the best answer.

1. Chutney, naan, and chai are from

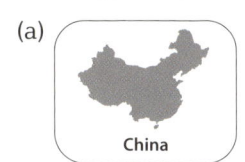

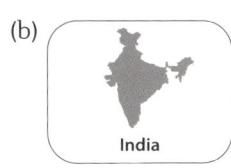

    (a) China (b) India (c) Australia

2. The word *naan* means "_____."

    (a) ingredients
    (b) sugar
    (c) bread

3. Chai is NOT made with

    (a) (b) (c)

Circle T (true) or F (false).

4. Naan is a type of dip.   T   F
5. Chai is often made on the street.   T   F
6. There is only one type of chutney.   T   F

Key: 1. (b) 2. (c) 3. (c) 4. (F) 5. (T) 6. (F)

27

New Words

- **breakfast** (n.) What do you eat for **breakfast**?
  ★ the foods we eat in the morning

- **clay** (n.) She is making a pot from **clay**.
  ★ a type of material from the ground

- **cook** (v.) Their job is to **cook** delicious food!
  ★ to make food and heat it so it is ready to eat

- **dip** (n.) We need more **dip** for the naan!
  ★ a type of sauce people put foods in to taste better

- **ingredient** (n.)   What **ingredients** do we need for dinner?
  - ★ one of the parts we need to make a food or a meal

- **billion** (n.)   **Billions** of people use the internet every day.
  - ★ 1,000,000,000

- **shape** (n.)   There are many **shapes** in the picture.
  - ★ the form of an object, such as a circle or square

- **spice** (n.)   The shop has lots of nice **spices**.
  - ★ something made from plants and added to foods to make them taste good

Little India

NAANS

Plain — $2

Garlic — $3

Peshwari — $4

VEGETARIAN DISHES

Dal makhani — $8
lentils cooked with butter and spices

Chana masala — $7
chickpeas with onions, tomatoes, garlic, and spices

MEAT DISHES

All meat dishes are served with rice and a variety of chutneys.

Butter chicken $11
cooked with butter and spices

Lamb rogan josh $12
cooked with onions, tomatoes, and spices

Chicken tikka kebab $12
pieces of chicken cooked in yogurt and spices

DESSERTS

Kheer $4
 rice pudding

DRINKS

Chai $3

Lassi *(Original / Mango flavor)* $3

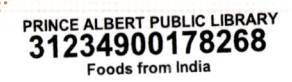

Notes

More words to use…

- with naan.

garlic

paneer

- with chutney.

cilantro

spicy

tomato

- with chai.

iced

cinnamon stick